EXHIBITION DESIGN
theory and practice

ARNOLD RATTENBURY

STUDIO VISTA: LONDON
VAN NOSTRAND REINHOLD COMPANY:
NEW YORK

A Studio Vista/Van Nostrand Reinhold Paperback
Edited by John Lewis
© Arnold Rattenbury 1971
All rights reserved
Published in London by Studio Vista Limited
Blue Star House, Highgate Hill, London N19
and in New York by Van Nostrand Reinhold Publishing
Company, a Division of Litton Educational Publishing, Inc.
450 West 33 Street, New York, NY 10001
Library of Congress Catalog Card Number: 75 151408
Set in 11 pt Baskerville 169 1 pt leaded
Printed and bound in the Netherlands
by Drukkerij Reclame N.V., Gouda
British ISBN 0 289.70008.6 (0 289.70009.4 hardback)

CONTENTS

PART ONE

THE OBJECT OF THE EXERCISE

A typical exhibition set-up, Olympia, London. Photograph: Lance Browne

I   WHAT EXHIBITIONS?

One needs some definition to start with, and while it would be properly ambitious and certainly exciting to gaze into a future of designing national exhibits for a Montreal or a Tokyo Expo, or re-designing interiors for the British Museum, or taking over a demolition site for a temporary exhibition in Detroit – all of which have been recent exhibition jobs – these pages will limit themselves to a far tighter definition than those ambitions suggest. For the immediate purpose, a working definition of exhibitions might be "the advertisement, in three dimensions, of a company's product or service."

I have put the words as flatly and as early as possible, not to deny anyone's proper ambition or put a damper on excitement, but to fix the position in which that ambition will almost certainly have to operate and that excitement grow. This is pre-eminently the area in which people will pay for exhibition design, and the name of it is not National Prestige or Public Need but Industry. Nor, for all that the definition is tight, is the area small. It is indeed colossal, and – though perforce one sees it most clearly from the country in which one works – worldwide.

For the period February–February 1970–1971, the London Bureau (Britain's centre of exhibition information) lists 275 "national" shows in the U.K., 115 of them in London, but with 10 or more occurring in Birmingham, Blackpool, Brighton, Dublin, Glasgow, Harrogate and Manchester, and covering 56 other towns. One says "national" in the sense that, while a particular exhibition in the list may sometimes be small – amounting perhaps to no more than a few dozen displays – it is nonetheless *the* show, the particular opportunity to exhibit nationally, rather than on a purely local basis, for producers within a given field. The list includes of course – and especially in London – many major "international" exhibitions: 37 of them claim the title, and another 20 or so deserve it on the grounds that overseas exhibitors habitually find them useful.

For the same period the same source lists 627 Overseas exhibitions in which its readers – in this case British businessmen, contractors and designers – may reasonably expect to become participants. Of these, 90 are in the United States: Chicago and New York 22 each; Philadelphia 7; Cleveland and Detroit 5 each; San Francisco 4; Anaheim, Denver and Houston 3 each; Baltimore, Miami and Washington 2 each; and 1 each in Atlantic City, Cincinnati, Las Vegas, Los Angeles, Louisville, New Orleans, Pittsburgh, Reading, Tampa and Tulsa. On the Continent, Berlin, Cologne, Dusseldorf, Frankfurt, Hamburg, Munich and Stuttgart together account for 59; Paris for 42; and the figures are comparably high for Belgium and the Netherlands, Canada, Holland, Italy, the Scandinavian countries and Spain. Japan, predictably, has jumped from a mere handful, ten or twelve, some years ago to over 40 now. But perhaps the biggest growth indicator is the way that numbers are rising for cities behind the Iron Curtain – Belgrade, Budapest, Kishinev, Leskovac, Ljubljana (8), Moscow (6), Plovdiv, Plzen, Poznan, Prague (8), Skopje, Warsaw, Zagreb (7) – and for cities in countries more recently emergent as major industrial markets – Accra, Addis Ababa, Beirut, Bulawayo, Izmir, Lima, Lusaka, Nairobi.

It is really a question of doing sums in the head in whatever country happens to be your base. Parallel American listings for Overseas shows would include the sixty or so "internationals" suggested above for the U.K. as being those in which American readers might reasonably expect to participate, and would correspond roughly – doubtless with some geographical adjustments to do with national trading and foreign policy – in respect of other countries. Despite Britain's traditional ties with Australia, for example, an American list would be stronger throughout the Australasian area. By the same token, its list for "national" shows would of course be infinitely higher than the mere 90 that figure on the British list.

But even all this listing of "nationals" and "internationals" is only the visible part of the iceberg above the waterline. One thinks of these as the major shows in any one country; but what, after all, makes a show "major" to the individual exhibitor?

The essence of all these listed exhibitions is that, by being Trade Shows of one kind and another, they are competitive: the exhibitor shows his product among rival products. But many manufacturers, and quite certainly many moments in all manufacture and marketing, don't ask for competitive showing. The exhibitor may wish to show, in conditions of absolute privacy, to his own "tied" dealers only. He may wish to show the purely development side of his work without the inevitable questions about availability and price, which he cannot yet answer, that would arise in a competitive show. He may be timorous, or new to a particular field of operation, and anxious to have a "dummy run" to test reaction.

The kind of venue he is likely to want for such occasions will be small – in Britain, more probably than not, an hotel where a modest show would not look lost, though the place may indeed be capable of mounting a "national" also. (No new hotel goes up these days without its inbuilt exhibition facilities.) Of the 115 exhibitions already quoted as listed for London, the locations of 21 during the twelve months February–February 1970–1971 are hotels. Checking round them at this time of writing, I find that between them they will in fact contain 32 shows in this month alone – a month for which a mere 2 are shown in the quoted list. Here, then, is one part of the iceberg below the waterline. There are others.

Both the American Chamber of Commerce and Britain's Board of Trade operate various schemes by which national manufacturers exhibit together abroad. Of their nature, these are often selective, space is not necessarily available in them on an ordinary application basis, and news about them is therefore not advertised and does not figure in lists. And increasingly, Exhibitions Organisers independent of government are operating similar schemes on their own. Or again, various kinds of self-crating re-use designs, while they do indeed move from one American State Fair or one British Agricultural Show to another, and therefore do become parts of listed "nationals" and "internationals", have also an existence independent of the lists, and are routed and programmed to appear on their own as individual promotions before, between and after their listed competitive appearances.

Particularly, then, in that very large area where Industry or Nation addresses itself in a specialised way and only initiator, designer, builder and invitee need ever hear of it, precise figures are hard to come by. But it is certainly quite common for anything between 50 and 90 per cent of the exhibition budget to which a designer is working for any one company to have nothing at all to do with "major" shows in the listed sense.

So the activity covered by even the narrow definition of exhibitions with which we started is both colossal and complex; and the complexity itself matters intensely to the designer. While it is comfortable to see the size of the thing, it is also essential to see it precisely for what it is, for from that nature stems a whole range of problems to be met persistently. Though we shall return to many of them many times later, imagine for the moment a simple quite arbitrary case.

The designer's introduction to a company has been, as is usual, to design one particular job within the year's programme. Suppose this represents 10 per cent of the company's annual exhibitions budget, and that this 10 per cent is totally inadequate to make the particularly brave show the company requires. Discussion between designer and client is on the general pattern of budget allocation.

Can something be saved there to add here?

Would the use of a single module between several different jobs offer a structural saving out of which a braver display might be afforded?

Even – should there be an overlap in dates of booking, for instance – should the actual programme be altered?

What anyway is the special importance of this show the designer is here to discuss?

How about that new show as an alternative?

What does the designer know about it?

Essentially this is the point. The client will know his own business: the designer had best know his; and in both cases the knowledge will run far wide of design and production, to include market, outlet and the whole ambience in which each operates. A discussion begun between them on a purely budgetary basis can easily extend to the whole matter of the company's exhibitions policy. Quite often a designer enters a meeting to discuss one particular job, and leaves without that job but with two others that are entirely different.

It isn't, then, merely a matter of studying lists and having a sense of what is missing from them. Constant visits to exhibition halls and contractors' works before and during set-up, continuing relationships with other clients (with other problems) and with organisers, combine into a general sense of movement within the exhibitions world. An old, apparently healthy annual show will often "feel" sickly long before it has opened: chief past exhibitors may be leaving it, or spending critically less on their stands. Or there may be a sudden shift in expenditure in one section of Industry, away from competitive trade shows altogether and into solus exhibitions: a contractor's works may be fuller than ever, though you have not seen him recently at the competitive locations. Or a new show will often "feel" successful months beforehand, simply because of the designer's odd snatched glances at the kinds of design and the kinds of money others are pouring into it.

Until an exhibition is dead, it is alive, and while it lives it changes. It is this sense of change, of how and why it happens, of where it looks like happening next, that the designer must develop. At times it may affect the actual programme on which he is employed. Invariably it comes to affect his design.

Only two hundred and fifty years ago that most prolix and enthusiastic of all prophets of factory production, Daniel Defoe, was reduced to a kind of apoplexy by the emergence of so small a hint of the Expos to come as the ordinary English shop.

"It is a modern custom and wholly unknown to our ancestors, who yet understood trade in proportion to the trade they carried on, as well as we do, to have tradesmen lay out two-thirds of their fortune in fitting up their shops.

"By fitting up, I do not mean furnishing their shops with wares and goods to sell; for in that they came up to us in every particular, and perhaps went beyond us too; but in painting and gilding, fine shelves, shutters, boxes, glass doors, sashes and the like, in which they tell us now, 'tis a small matter to lay out two or three hundred pounds, nay, five hundred pounds, to fit up a pastry cook's, or a toy shop.

"It will hardly be believed in ages to come, when our posterity shall be grown wiser by our loss, and, as I may truly say, at our expense, that a pastry cook's shop, which twenty pounds would effectively furnish at a time, with all needful things for sale, yet that fitting up one of these shops should cost upwards of 300 *l*, Anno Domini, 1710, let the year be recorded."

Like Canute, Defoe sat before a tide that did not, for all his hopefulness, recede. The world he was born into was one in which like trades congregated together – silk at Spitalfields, broadlooms at Halifax, watchmaking at Clerkenwell, cutlery at Sheffield, sailmaking at Tower Hamlets, stockings at Nottingham, and so on. You went to one area for one particular product, and precisely because it was a defined area, comparisons of price and quality and the possibilities of competition essential to trade were in-built.

But the very industrialisation Defoe so much and so prophetically applauded changed more than he knew. The land off which men had lived was enclosed; cities – even, by emigration, nations – grew and became industrial cities and industrial nations, but the new industrial proletariat was still closely related to a pastoralism which had no Main Street U.S.A., no High Street U.K., but functioned by fair and market and a form of barking-busking salesmanship. These pastoral fairground habits persisted, and still persist, long after the disappearance of any visible pasture.

This matters to the contemporary designer. "Comparisons of price and quality and the possibilities of competition" remain important: similar manufactures must show themselves together. Yet salesmanship still has something of fairground about it. Much liquor flows at almost every exhibition, lights flash on and off, motorcars spin like merry-go-rounds, and dolly girls are everywhere. The great popular success of Prince Albert's Great Exhibition of 1851 can thus he seen as one huge embodiment of both these needs. With its Crystal Palace and fireworks and bandstands and exotica and deliberate bid for a new consumer-public it was an enormous fair in the pastoral sense; with its careful division into industrial sections, it would have rejoiced the heart of Defoe.

The difference is of course that we are no longer townsman or countryman in that old sense, but both at once. The division is not between two factions in the exhibitions world – one solemn, competitive, dry-as-dust, and the other frivolous – but within all of us, the client, the designer, the organiser, and the man in the street who comes into the exhibition through its turnstiles. The man who elected to show his car alongside his rival manufacturers' cars is also the man who decreed that there should be a dolly sitting on its bonnet. For every Trade Exhibition that is called a Trade Exhibition, there are two called Trade Fairs and three called Trade Shows. Nor is this simply a play on words. The conception of showing manufacture in such a way as to enhance

16

its actual virtues is constantly entangled with the conception of
having fun. The two of course are not inimical, but they do determine much that is typical of all exhibition work and how that
work changes.

The original intention is almost always specialised: a section of
Industry wishing to shows its wares to that specialised section of
the public which is its market. If the show succeeds, it grows.
Attendances grow. With a captive audience other related sections
of Industry begin to exhibit and to attract in their turn their own
specialised sections of the public. Since the "general public" is
only another way of describing every specialised section added
together, there comes a point when the original intention is lost
and the show is in danger of becoming merely another annual
Bean Feast. That is the moment when groups of exhibitors begin
to decide that interest is now so diffuse that they must either have
another new exhibition of their own or go on their own and
exhibit solo.

Every successful exhibition is in this way a sow in farrow, every
new one the moment at which an old one can no longer support
a body of its exhibitors. From a Furniture show is born a Contract
Furniture exhibition, a Carpet exhibition, a Bedding Centre, a
Do-it-Yourself show, a Furniture Manufacturers fair, even the
decision to open a major showroom of one's own and be done with
exhibitions for good; from an Office Equipment exhibition is
born a Business Efficiency fair, and in turn from that a Computer
show; and I will go bail that at this moment the major international Plastics exhibitions of Germany, the United States and
Britain are all of them in farrow, so diverse a number of specialised interests do Plastics now serve.

Except in the very new-born exhibition, where the first intention remains baby-simple, the client and his designer are always
at a point of greater or lesser tension between the specialised and
the general in this way. So long as the public attendance can be

foretold with reasonable precision, it is sensible enough for a stand design to be open and clamouring for attention – even raucous. The troubles come later. Will too successful a come-all-ye approach in fact bring running a crowd of the unwanted, simply because too many of the unwanted are in the hall? Will an austere and enclosed design, however prestigious, freeze out potential new customers? In order to "think" a design in the first place, the designer has to develop some sense of the point in all this shift of patterns that his particular show has reached.

Nothing better illustrates the client's and designer's point of tension I have tried to describe than the way in which Exhibition Organiser companies operate; and they *are* companies, in precisely the sense of the exhibitor's company, in business for profit.

Once they have taken over the running of an existing exhibition, or set about the safe delivery of a new one, they book a location and date for it. They issue a brochure for those they hope will exhibit. They may call a launching conference to test and encourage support. They employ consultant engineers for survey and overall plans of the venue. They become involved in the issue of rules and regulations that have to vary from show-to-show, simply because the nature of exhibits varies. Necessarily at an early stage they have fixed a cost-per-foot or cost-per-metre rental which they will charge the exhibitors for sites; and before that stage they will have had designed and costed a "shell scheme", enabling exhibitors to avoid structural work, and issued a cost-per-foot for that at the same time. They are involved in fact, before a single exhibitor's booking exists, in an enormous capital outlay – for location, for consultants, designers, printwork, costing staff, circularisation. There is infinitely more expense to come for them; and against it all they have two sources of income only: the site rentals, and the "gate".

There are of course ways to control the "gate". Nowadays it is customary for the organiser to sell the exhibitor personal invitation tickets which offer at least the chance that the particular kinds of person the exhibitor wishes to attract will be included whoever else gets in. Or indeed, provided exhibitors will wear the need for far higher site rentals, by cutting out the "gate" as a source of income to the organiser, entry can be restricted to invitation only. Alternatively, the "gate" price can be fixed so high that only those with a truly specialised interest, it is argued, will pay it; but especially where the exhibition's subject is new – automative, say, or computerised – the general pull to see "the

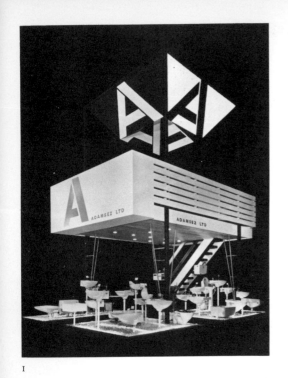

1

2

Four stands from a series by the same designer for the same client at the same exhibition (Buildex, London), showing how shifts in the pattern of attendance can affect design.

1 1959: public access to exhibits is limited by standing them on underlit glass marbles. The totally enclosed upper deck is for business.
2 1961: a "stockade" encloses but reveals both decks, inhibiting casual visitors but inviting the serious.
3 1963: the exhibits are now easily accessible at ground level, but the upper deck remains entirely enclosed.
4 1965: now a single-decker in a show with a highly specialised attendance, virtually the whole stand is open for business amongst the exhibits.

Designer: *Donald Dewar-Mills*. Contractors: 1959 B & S Displays Ltd, 1961 Cockade Ltd, 1963 and 1965 F. W. Clifford Ltd.

20

3

4

wonders of the age" (as they used to be called in pastoral fairgrounds) remains a powerful thing, and totally unspecialised members of the public will pay, and in droves, to see what is quite beyond their understanding.

Exhibition organisers customarily circularise exhibitors with a list of "approved" contractors as a guide to the inexperienced. Experienced exhibitors, even those with their own design departments, will know the work of many contractors and designers already and quite possibly employ a panel of independent outsiders to ring the changes on style. Few contractors contain their own design departments, operating instead a loose but productive relationship with designers whose work they know from previous building. Experienced or inexperienced, the exhibitor may put the whole of his exhibitions programme in the hands of his advertising or public relations agency; and there, too, the recent tendency has been for agencies to close their special departments for stand design and rely on personal, informal relationships much as do the contractors. Insofar as I can trace the source of jobs as an independent designer, mine have come in the main from contractors or agencies, and far less often from a satisfied client informing a rival or from having produced a palpable miracle on site.

The source of a designer's work is ultimately of course the exhibitor, the client. But whose client? The contractor's? The agency's? His own? Sooner or later, and for reasons to which most of this book is devoted, the answer has to be "his own", for there is no other way to cope with a client's problems than by direct contact. But too often designers forget that contractor and agency, too, will be claiming the client as their own; and the designer may easily find himself therefore, particularly with his contractor, regarded with suspicion and as an interloper.

The only thing the contractor may know about him is that he is currently working with six other contractors on other jobs; and there may be a justifiable fear – it has happened often enough – that the designer will take the client elsewhere next time. Or unfamiliarity with the designer's drawing-style, his "shorthand", may lead to misunderstandings about what exactly has been costed. The point in essence is simple. The client has employed them both, and if the design is going to work then this is the contractor who is going to make it work; and just as the contractor will have to familiarise himself with the designer's "short-hand", so the designer had better familiarise himself with the particular talents and skills and conventions that operate here, adapt his drawing-style if need be, supplement drawings with additional detail sheets perhaps, and double-check all costings.

All successful exhibiting is a collective effort, and the good jobs come of a complete collaboration, however hard it may sometimes be to achieve.

PART TWO   THE PEOPLE INVOLVED

5   DESIGNER AND CLIENT

In a major industrial company with a considerable exhibitions programme there may be a department whose whole business is progressing that programme – the supply of exhibits and special photography to stands, relations with organisers, designers and contractors, arranging specialist attendences and so on – and even where this is not the case, the programme will be under the control of an exhibitions manager of considerable experience. So múch the better. Such people know what they want, are familiar with all the possible conflicts of appeal and function in any exhibition, and above all have an intimate sense of cost and the possibilities of budget. But they are rare.

The designer is far more likely to find himself among people who do not habitually think in three-dimensional terms. These may be a Sales Manager, an Advertising Manager, perhaps a Company Director whose personal baby this relatively extra-ordinary form of expenditure, an exhibition, has become. The designer may meet them separately or together. He will almost certainly find himself caught up in what seems the perennial rivalry between Sales and Advertising. Even such simple questions as "Why are you going into this exhibition? What do you hope to get out of it?" will very frequently receive such bewildering and unhelpful answers as "Well, we always have" or "Blessed if I know". Arriving to receive a brief, he may find in fact that he has to provide it himself. It is for this reason that the earlier chapters of this book matter. The designer is the one who knows exhibitions, the direction in which the one at issue is moving, the possibilities of impact, the likelihoods of swamping specialist interest under a wash of general appeal, and so on. Such clients can only add to this their own intimate knowledge of their company's product and service; and while the designer most certainly needs that knowledge, only by asking and listening and prodding can he construct a set of aims that his three-dimensional thinking can reasonably hope to achieve on the client's behalf.

1

2

3

1 Presentation to client has been by a hinged model showing both enclosed and open detail as visual presentation could not have done (Chapter 13). The model is now checked with drawings by the contractor.
2 The same drawing in use in the shop where fascias are being made.
3 The fascia being erected on site. Simplicity and economy in drawing is essential where so many different people are to use it (Chapter 14).

Designer: *Geoff Butcher;* Contractor, K Displays and Exhibitions Ltd.

The completed stand shown at various stages on previous pages.

Slightly less common than this sort of under-briefing is a habit of over-briefing: the production of a list of requirements, even sometimes of sketches, so various and contradictory that they cannot conceivably be compressed into either the available space or budget. Once again, the designer must abstract from this the bold outlines of a working brief, distinguishing main from subsidiary aims, function from appearance, movement and use from the column-inch view of advertising or the stock-shelf view of sales, three dimensions from two.

The bulk of initial briefings are of this under-or-over kind; but the lack of the third dimension in them, while it certainly means that the client is not thinking in exhibition terms in one sense, equally does not mean that he is not thinking about exhibitions at all. What the designer must discover – and now, at the earliest possible stage – is *what,* if anything, his client is thinking about them. Any client, however austerely commercial he may seem, is likely to contain one way or another some sense of fun and occasion. Almost certainly it won't match the designer's, and almost certainly – since this is, after all, a solemn business meeting – it won't be expressed. There will however be pointers. The decision may have gone against having a bar in the "discussion area", but now is the time to discover whether or not to provide an extra lock-up cupboard for what the client will almost certainly call "the odd bottle". The designer may have taken a detailed list of every illustration the stand requires, but now is the time to discover whether there is to be space left blank for "the odd picture of the President's (or the Queen's, or Miss World's) visit to the Works". Or if there is to be "the odd dolly" decorating the stand, to note that she will need at least a cubby-hole with a mirror in it. More critically, now is the time to discover whether or not the client shares that very general passion among exhibitors for floral decoration, for this is a passion that cannot be hidden by walls.

In the end, the success of any design for a stand that is "going to work" depends in large part on those who are there to work it. What these businessmen facing the designer now regard as proper to exhibitions, what makes them operate in comfort, is certainly one factor in the brief you take back to the drawingboard. Build the flowers in from the start, or talk them out from the start, but don't ignore them.

The startling difference between this type of meeting and one with a client who has not exhibited before is that here there will at least be a realistic sense of budget. Last year's costs will be known and therefore what was once achieved for what. It is as useless to leave a briefing meeting without a definite sense of what the client will spend as it is to attend one without at least a hunch about the general costs of structures and display, the habit called "guesstimate". No clarity about what the design must do is worth a light without an equal clarity about how it is to be afforded. Is the client himself, or the contractor's budget which you are spending for him, to include your fees; the cost of photo blow-ups and caption-setting, or is he to supply the negatives; the transport of his exhibits, and their fixing, or is that to come out of budget? The designer must find out not only what the budget is, but what precisely it is to cover. For the new exhibitor it may be the designer's difficult task to make clear to him just how much an exhibition costs.

The new exhibitor, on the other hand, may well be far more explicit about what he wants and may even give a better brief. He has made a unique decision to book a site at a rental that interferes considerably with his ordinary advertising programme, and is probably already aware that the supply of exhibits to a stand will also interfere with the normal functioning of his production and delivery lines. His misfortune is that he may have done this because, as a visitor to this same exhibition the year before, he saw the kinds of impact that can be achieved without costing them. In the U.K. in 1971 it is the case that at £5 or £6 a square foot you can – you do not always – achieve a good deal more in the way of impact than at £2, below which you can hardly go. The designer may have to explain that no house in perpetuity (though it may cost no more) is papered with excess-size photo blow-ups, or lit like a beacon, or prints and then publishes upon its walls book-loads of information, or contains glazed walls, custom made metal objects, fibreglass murals, poly-styrene, mobiles, backlighting, motorised models, or is furnished by hire at prices very near purchase, or lit on the same basis, or above all is put together in perhaps as little as twentyfour hours to be both solid and yet dismantleable in less.

The meetings I have described are all first ones, but likely to be the only ones until the actual submission of a design. Though other clients met for the first time may not seem like any of these characters, basically they are. Within them all, as it seems to me, are quirks, prejudices, false assumptions, that must seem odd to the designer (though probably no odder than the designer's, about Industry, to them).

Meetings between designer and organiser are normally few but can be crucial. The probability is that once the designer is acting for the client a site has already been fixed; the possibility, that there is even now some choice available. Factors affecting this choice may be: varying rentals; the advantages of a small but prime site in the sense of commanding better and more open approach views, weighed against a more distant but larger site; or even the ability to achieve a projected design due to rules that may restrict the building-height, floor-loading, availability of water-and-waste, or access routes for some particularly large exhibit. They are most likely to be matters of choice between "shell scheme" and "breakaway" sites: that is to say, sites on which the design is for the interior of a supplied structure only, or sites on which the designer is free to go higher, possibly wider and a good deal more handsome with his structure.

Client and designer together can quite happily decide on all these matters without reference to the organiser, simply by reference to their own past experience of the exhibition in question; and it is indeed quite common for the designer to have no more communication with the organiser than the submission of plans for approval. There is however a vast area of "waivers" and "special permissions" which the designer can reach with the organiser on his client's behalf, and which may free his design and let it live and work in ways not otherwise possible.

The argument for "shell schemes", for example, is triple-pronged: a large area built to a standard module makes it possible for the organiser to offer essential site-bounding walls, floor and ceiling more cheaply than each exhibitor alone would be able to acquire them; an equality of impact is imposed on all alike so that the wealthier neighbouring exhibitor cannot simply blind your client out of existence with some costly and startling edifice the more orderly street-like appearance of "shell scheme" areas are themselves perhaps a help to visitors, conducive to business

therefore, and help to impose the ⌐
individual images. Clearly, for the first pa⌐
work, the "shell scheme" has to be built as one a⌐
is intended to reach a stand already at one stage of co⌐
The intention is not, however, to restrict the uses to which ⌐
"shell" can then be put.

The client may wish for water-and-waste, or for wiring, to run under the floor to some working exhibit. He may have a corner-site which nonetheless includes a side wall, and may wish to lose it in favour of extra diagonal approach-view. Or he may wish to gain it, where the "shell scheme" has left it off, in order to gain more wall display. Intervals between supporting posts to the facia may hamper his freedom to locate exhibits on the front of his stand. He may wish to replace a post with an equally support-ing story-board of his own. On a site with very long frontage an absolutely uninterrupted view may be important to him, and he would like his facia suspended rather than ground-supported. All these are matters which can, or can't, be settled by the designer arranging the necessary waivers with the organiser.

The situation for "breakaway" sites is essentially the same. The organiser's "Rules and Regulations" governing them, and almost certainly governed in the last resort by local authority safety and fire precautions, may forbid building above a certain height; but a designer may well propose a feature above that height on part of the stand space, which is neither unsafe nor (what will be in the organiser's mind) seriously obscures anyone's view of neighbouring stands. This, and an almost infinite number of other special permissions, the organiser may well be disposed to allow; and the designer can but try him.

The point is that if he leaves such matters until after the accept-ance of a design by his client, and after its costing and the award of contract, he is in line to reap a whirlwind of disappointments and revisions of his own making – where god knows, as later chapters should make clear, he is in for enough already. Far better take it that the organiser is at least as reasonable as himself, as anxious to keep his clients happy, and make a friend of the man – however like boa constrictors his "Rules and Regulations" may sometimes appear.

A decreasing number of stand-fitting contractors are large concerns employing more than 70 or 80, sometimes more than 100 staff; most employ between 30 and 50; and the rest, who are difficult to count because of their propensity to vanish, employ a dozen and sometimes less. Most of these small firms have been founded by skilled workers from inside an existing outfit. They are almost all enthusiastic about their work, and virtually inexhaustible – as indeed they have need to be. In the large contracting firms, actual directorship, as with any other sizeable business, is likely to be by a professional director, an accountant perhaps, a businessman *tout court*. The designer will deal with his sales representative or head of department.

Therein lies the essential difference between big and middle. The large company may well contain, in addition to carpenters' shop, paintshop, spraying room, display shop (which the "middles" will also contain), a metalworks, a silkscreen shop, a photographic department, possibly also type-setting facilities, a drawing office, and almost certainly individuals skilled in working polystyrene, making models, using foils and fibreglass and other special materials. Even if all these are not within one works, the volume of jobs put out by that contractor will give him a privileged, position with specialist sub-contractors. One cannot say that nothing is impossible to him – in an exhibitions world in which emergency and panic are endemic, nothing can be impossible to anyone – but it must be less impossible to him than to others. On the other hand his overheads are greater and, although at the time of writing I do not find big company prices higher, they sometimes have been in the past and could be again. He also has the advantage, when tendering in competition, that he could presumably better afford to undercut his prices to secure a particularly desirable client: a situation the designer would be wise to watch, or a second stand for the same client could seem expensive after a first secured by such a method.

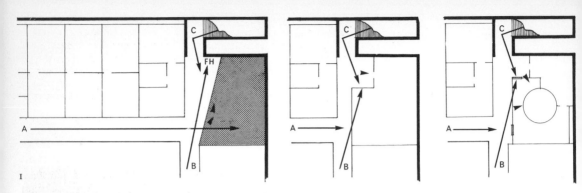

I

2

Three examples of waivers (special permissions) arranged by designers with organisers on their clients' behalf.

1 Access to the fire hydrant (FH) was essential, but the original shaded site gave poor approach views (A, B). The designer's request narrowed the gangway too much, but provided the basis for the vastly improved approach views of the site as finally agreed, right.

2 An obligatory "shell scheme" line pushed back to allow the use of a client's existing re-use units on the site perimeters.

3 A roof feature clad with client's exhibits hoisted above the permitted building height, represented by the rear wall, in a dead-end site where this could not interfere with other exhibitors.

3

The "middles" are critically different. Among the directors may be men who have recently been a joiner on the bench and a practising sign-writer; a metalworker, a designer and a display man; two carpenters; a man who has recently been exhibition-buyer for a large corporation, a display man and a carpenter.* In such circumstances, the Managing Director is quite likely to take the visiting designer across to the carpenter's bench, pick up a saw, and physically demonstrate some possible improvement or economy to a detail in the design. Especially in terms of economy this kind of episode is useful. By the time a job is progressing through works, the client may well be adding "extras", the costs of which the designer would like to minimise. But there are dangers too. At this kind of late stage, the designer is unlikely to confirm this kind of amendment in drawing; and a particularly delicate amendment requires that the actual carpenter to do the work is as skilled as his Managing Director.

If the special emergency which has brought the designer to works belongs, let us say, to metalwork, and if that is out in a sub-contractor's works on the other side of town, or in another town, one is not, for all this willingness, much further forward.

Essentially the problem here, where the "middle" contractor has perhaps no stable relationship with one metalworks or one photographer, is to know exactly what the contractor's potential is, and to put his way only such work as is reasonably within it. If there is metal in the design, then let it be well clear of what the designer's worst fears anticipate the client may change. If the photographic work is complex, the designer might be advised to split the contract and place it, and watch its progress, separately. What the designer can in no wise do is lay the blame later for what he could have noticed sooner.

* These are all directoral boards with which I have worked.

With the small contractor, the case is the same but more so. He will have fewer skills at his disposal and a greater proportion of the work will go out to sub-contractors. Two carpenters, a painter and a labourer, if that is what he has available on site for instance, will not stretch far. The skills and the enthusiasms may be the same – and some jobs will be within his competence, some well outside it (though he will optimistically quote for all). But he may, just possibly, be cheap on a job where for various reasons cheapness is all and time is not of its essence. In the end the problem is always the same. The design must match, or be made to match by however many sheets of detailed amendments may prove necessary, the contractor's competence; and for that the designer has to know the competence. There is no substitute therefore for visiting contractor's works, whether or not there is work to be placed immediately, or for watching progress on site on other stands than the designer's own.

From the start, client and designer will have discussed the placing of contract, and have probably decided for a three- or four-way competition, a contractor particularly favoured by the client being among the competitors. Or the client may simply dump the whole business of selecting a contractor in the designer's lap, recognising (he had better be right) that the designer is more knowledgeable in this matter than himself. There is never any sense in the designer not putting the drawings to competitive tender, and a good deal of commonsense safeguard, to both designer and client, in doing so.

The position can therefore vary anywhere between knowing beyond any doubt who is going to get the job anyway, and knowing that you can virtually pick your man yourself. These extremes, and the very wide range of possibilities between them, existing before the design does, might well themselves become yet another factor determining that design.

The like point in all these situations is that price alone should not be, and very rarely is, the sole determining factor in the award of contract. Happy existing client-contractor associations are beyond price. A designer's conviction that so-and-so above all others has the skills to interpret perfectly some aspect of his scheme can be decisive. A design involving a lot of pre-fixing of client's exhibits in works may well militate in favour of a contractor near the client's factory though far from the exhibition location. On the other hand, if there are to be many last minute amendments, it may be essential to employ a contractor whose works are near the exhibition site. What the designer must have is absolute confidence that what he designs is within the contractor's competence to make. There is no more harrowing moment for him than the late (too late) discovery that some long, important, unbroken timber feature is arriving in sections on site simply because the contractor's workshed, or even perhaps his transport, could not deal with it physically in the intended way. A designer must build up a knowledge of the potentials of as many contractors as possible.

The skills required in exhibition work are immense and have to be applied with great speed. Six years ago I watched a craftsman hanging speedily and to perfection William Morris's "Blackthorn" wallpaper down the underside of a descending spiral, with wet emulsion paint on his flank and still greasy metals rising from the spiral.

I have not seen that craftsman since, and he may for all I know have left the exhibitions world. But if I find he is in it still, then the contractor for whom he works, of whatever size, is one I shall watch with particular care, for that may prove to be a contractor valuing exceptional skills and able to keep his craftsmen happy.

PART THREE   THE DESIGNER'S EXERCISE

8   THE BUDGET AND RE-USE

Certain areas of cost can be fixed at once. The designer will know, whether the stand is to be platformed and carpeted or covered in some other way over-all. The site location, with or without neighbouring sites butting or backing to it, will determine the number of essential party-walls and whether they need be double- or single-clad. The brief, or common caution, may suggest that the stand be roofed. (It is the fact, and he will know it, that pigeons nest and the rest inside the roofs of many major exhibition venues.) A plumbing point may be required. Even so early as this, and despite the possibility of special electrical effects in the eventual design, it could be sensible to calculate a cost figure for general lighting and motored machinery, if any. Depending of course upon the generosity of the budget, between a quarter and a half of it can easily have gone already.

The point about the kinds of item I have listed is that there isn't much to be done about them. Contractors, generally, hold stocks of wall-panels and, in the U.K. where flooring and under-floor wiring are the convention, of floor-flaps. Wall-panels, again in the U.K. though measurements elsewhere are of course to metric standards, are usually $8' \times 4'$, sometimes $9' \times 4'$, softwood $2'' \times 1''$ frameworks faced on one side or both with hardboard to form single- or double-clad units, depending on whether one or both sides will be visible. I have seen $36'$ of such walling go up in $4^1/_4$ minutes – not to be beautiful, but to function, and quickly.

Like floor-flaps and wall-panels, the lowest common denominator of exhibition ceiling – muslin stapled to battens – is at an almost universal fixed cost. So are light fittings, whose fixture can in the main only be carried out on site by "approved contractors", whose prices again are near enough identical, though the range of styles may vary. On a tight budget therefore, where flooring, walling, ceiling and lighting of some sort have to happen, this kind of quartering or halving of budget, however disas-

I

A re-use design consisting of floor, ceiling and fascia units, the locking devices between which also hold verticals, in turn holding interchangeable walls and display. Intended chiefly for overseas use, the parts are light, without screws or movable parts, simple enough for erection by unskilled local labour and flexible in layout.

1 & 2 Show the assembly of floor units and verticals at Tokyo.

2

trous it may seem, will almost certainly leave more money for the designer to think with than would be left were the whole structure to be custom-built. It also follows that not the least advantage of the looser budget is that it permits such a startling simplicity to exhibitions as a plain wall higher and wider than 9′ × 4′, not covered with wood chip paper endeavouring to hide the often lurid past of a contractor's stock wall-panels.

47

3

3 & 4 The same units at Tokyo showing infill panels and fascias.

4

5

6

5 The stand completed at Auckland, New Zealand.
6 The stand completed at London.
7 The stand completed at Toronto, Canada.

Designer: *Harry Amson;* Main Contractor, Cooke's (Finsbury) Ltd.

7

Such stock is normally on hire from the contractor. It might seem sensible to adopt a different system and encourage the client to buy outright. Briefing meetings will frequently produce the suggestion that, for the sake of some element good and important enough for future re-use, the client would in principle be willing to go over the budget. Why not extend the principle? For instance, a 36' wall might have been formed by screwing a metal U-section to the floor and dropping into it a series of H-section verticals, into the receiving sides of which standard sheets of blockboard or any other suitable surface might be slotted. Surely this might cost the client more than hiring in the first place, but a second use would cost him infinitely less. There is a sort of snag-filled truth in this.

How often is the client going to exhibit? Is the designer working on a year's programme entailing use, say, every two months; or is the client a twice-a-year exhibitor only? The essence of the argument for outright purchase is that no-one needs a 2" wall for a fortnight's stability: 1" or less will do. The essence of the answer is that 1" or less will develop the bends, or go mouldy, or have its finish peel away when not in use. And who is to store it? The contractor, whose space is likely to be at a premium and who must surely charge a storage rental? The client? But this is a client, let us suppose, who exhibits rarely; and he is being asked not only to store units but to keep them in re-usably good condition – something probably quite outside the other duties of his company's storekeepers. And anyway are you preserving something worth preserving? The finish to these walls will carry display, colour, wording, photography. Who can guarantee that the slogans under which the client sells, the pictures he wishes to show, the colour-scheme that pleased him once, even his company's logo and lettering style, will remain as useful to him for the next show as for this? Economies reached this way can prove phenomenally false.

There are occasions on which this kind of thinking about brief and budget indubitably pays. In a booking-plan through a series of State Fairs, for example, it is practically inevitable – for factors of time alone – that everything should be on a shove-up-tear-down-shove-up-again basis. Not dissimilarly, if a client has briefed the designer for a show in March and another in May, and if the designer adds the budgets together and comes up with the answer that, on a re-use basis, the client might well afford a third (if there is one suitable) in April at virtually no contractual cost, there would indeed be a case to put. The client will have his site-rental and staffing costs, of course, and the cost of extra dislocation to his business, and may be right to deny the case. He will be infinitely less likely to do so if the designer's proposal is for units which, while they look after shows in March and May, might also be used in private promotions in hotels of the kind mentioned in Chapter 1, or do duty as smaller showroom displays in an interim. Both client and designer will also have a boredom factor to contend with: over longer periods than, say, March to September they certainly will. The units will lose their freshness and excitement to the client and his staff – and the client may come to exaggerate the extent to which this boredom factor might affect his public.

Elements within a design can certainly be re-used – usually items of display, light-boxes, murals, even sometimes such structural elements as verticals between which the module of load-bearing platforms or spanning banners can be altered on re-use – but experience, not only of one's own work but of the look of companies whose flirtations with re-use one has followed, suggests that the boredom factor, changes in fashion, wear-and-tear, most clients' liking to be "different", not from themselves last month so much as from their competitors, to date continue to load the emphasis towards cost-per-stand and away from cost-per-series.

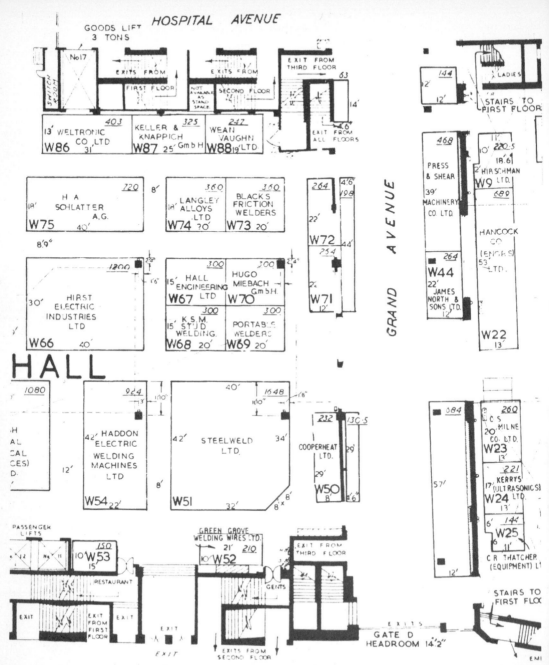

Part of a typical exhibition site drawing at the scale (1/400) at which the designer will probably see it first.

At an early stage the organiser will have posted each client a booking plan. This bird's eye view, locating the site, distinguishing broad from narrow gangways, suggesting the most likely angles of public approach and patterns of visitor-flow, giving approximate dimensions, is useful and may indeed have been used at the briefing meeting to suggest a particular concentration of display at some critical point. But if this is the only plan the designer has, it will not do. With the best eyes and rulers in the world it seems sometimes 65′, sometimes 66′ to the inch, sometimes at no constant scale at all. Now that the designer is actually tackling the job it needs to be insisted – if only because it is so often forgotten – that bird's eye views are strictly for the birds!

The better-organised exhibitions will have confirmed the booking with a dyeline print of a proper drawing at 32′ to the inch (or 1/400 metricated) – perhaps at a better scale for the smaller show. This is almost invariably a photo-reduction of a drawing at 16′ to the inch (1/200 metricated) prepared professionally for the organiser by his consulting engineers. This will generally be very accurate and contain keyed information about structural pillars, water, waste, fire hydrants, exits, loading areas, access dimensions, floor tolerances, power supply, and possibly section details.

But even this information has its disadvantages. A pencil line, at 32′ to the inch, is a foot thick. Photo-reduction may have fuzzed it to eighteen inches or more. The original negative may have been printed many times, amended, scratched, torn, been taped over, or even scattered with ash; and many things may print as structures that aren't and many actual structures be obscured. Printing may not have picked up every pillar and, on a drawing of such evenly distributed detail, a pillar may easily have been omitted in the draughting. In a long run of prints, some will be very mottled and blue. The often complicated walls of Victorian and Edwardian buildings used for exhibitions are often cluttered

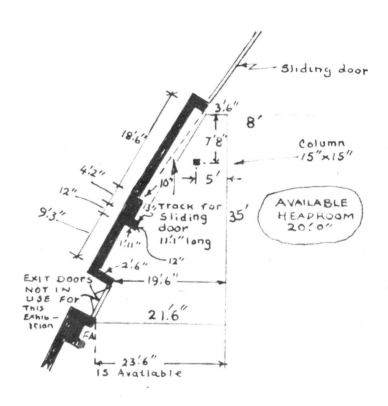

Typical details, at actual size, available on request from most organisers' consulting engineers. None of the complexity of measurements (left) or of available underfloor services (right) can be shown on site plans; and both may radically affect design.

Consulting Engineer: *Ian J. M. Bland*, T.D., M.A. (Cantab), C.Eng., M.I.Mech. E., M.Cons.E.

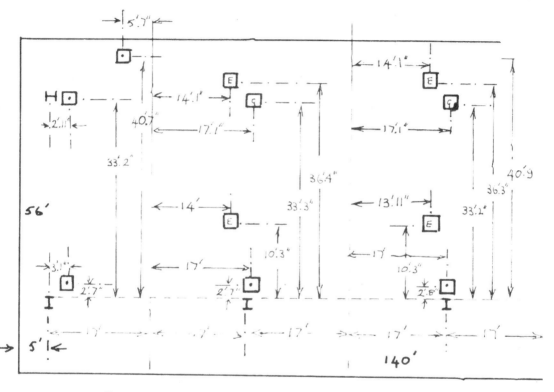

FLOORBOXES.

◻ DRAINS 2'10" sq.

E ELECTRIC 2'7" sq.

G GAS, WATER & WASTE 2'10" sq.

57

up with miles of piping, ducting, knotted with vents, junction-boxes and stop-cocks, none of which can even be indicated on a foot-thick pencil-line. If the stand-fitting building height in the "Rules and Regulations" is to be 10′ and if a major duct appears below this height, the consulting engineer in making his drawing is in some quandary. He will probably draw it in on plan, where it can only be read as floor-to-ceiling, though it may in fact only start at 9′ high. No general information can be shown for the possibilities of suspension, though these are almost always available. Possible misreadings and omissions are only too likely.

If you and the organiser are both in Birmingham or Los Angeles, you can at least call round and see his master drawing at 16′ to the inch. This will have been less often printed and be less scarred or fuzzed than your own, but it will not give you information it never contained. In any case you may be in Birmingham and the organiser in Los Angeles. In most cases the organiser, or better still the consulting engineer direct – his name will be on the drawing – will supply a detailed sketch of your particular stand or clear your mind in some simpler, verbal way: "There are no obstructions of any kind at that point below a height of 14′″, perhaps, or "The whole of that wall is a tangle of pipes and you ought to set your panels forward 9″ along its whole length", or "The whole of that wall is a tangle of pipes, but your site has already been set forward 9″ from it."

In the long run of course, experience teaches and familiarity with at least the major exhibition halls breeds not only contempt – for a lot of them are surely contemptible – but a lot of know-how. By far the most worthwhile chore to undertake is to visit earlier exhibitions and make for the area of the site you are to occupy and case it. (This you will have to do if there is no professional site drawing). You may even discover that the building brackets, which prevent that overhead structure you so much wish to erect, are only a foot or so wrong for you. You may be able to persuade the organiser into the slight adjustment necessary to put you right when he comes to chalk the hall out to receive contractors. (In this way, the chalkman once set a whole gangway of stands forward 6″ for me to allow a backlit box to appear flush on my one little stand's rear wall. He didn't mind: he had ten gangways in which to lose 6″; but it's another case where personal contact helped.)

The kinds of thing which familiarity with site can avoid for you are horrible to contemplate, but you should: pre-fabricated double-decker stands, whose upper floor has to be refabricated during set-up on site because it tangles with the building's roof; a "skylon" vertical feature 24′ high, which has to be cut in half because there is nowhere the necessary arc through which it must be hoisted, and then must be strained from the roof because the central joint is weak; the waste-pipe from a sink for which the nearest trap is under the floor of a completed stand two sites away. And none of these is the worst of them.

There is another sense in which you can know your site.

For diplomatic reasons of various sorts, the organiser does not always like to publish to all exhibitors the state of bookings in the early stages. There may be a shortage of big names. A notorious enemy of your client may look like becoming his neighbour. In a sectionalised show where, let us imagine, light units are separated from heat units, and both from sound units, the sectionalisation may be breaking down and producing an ill-assorted section. The organiser may well be less reticent with the designer, who also doesn't wish his client to withdraw, than with the client himself; and a knowledge of who the neighbours and facers are likely to be can radically affect design. The man on the right may have the good bleak habit of always showing in black and white settings. The man opposite might be given to a plenitude of little light-boxes. The man behind may retain a designer you know, and you may be able to liaise with him towards some mutual economy in rear-wall structure. Particularly in the case of a "bad" site, far down a narrow gangway with only squint-views possible from any main concourse, almost any knowledge of what is likely to be happening along the sides of the squint can much determine how you think the design you are now considering.

Enough has been said already about the need for contractors to subcontract on almost any design; and enough is generally known about the commonsense practice of businesses, to realise that sub-contraction must involve a considerable area of on-cost. There will be charges for *not* doing the work, for putting it out but controlling it. The temptation for the designer to place the sub-contracts direct himself can therefore be considerable, since this must "ease" the budget.

The fact of the matter is however that there has to be some simple single ultimate responsibility, and no designer that I have ever met can afford to live on site. His primary duty is to see that the design can work, and that his eventual drawings indeed ensure that brick, slate, wood, cork, perspex, 2″ tube, and the rest all meet where they are supposed to meet. One can only speak as one finds. I used to split the contract a lot: I don't now, unless compelled. The decisive element is that of time, since splitting the contract leads to a mass of extra work.

Different contractors need different drawings. Design has become Liaison, the amount of double-checking involved is enormous. On-cost, which started it all, may in the end seem cheap at the price. And it is anyway doubtful how the designer stands in charging for this not strictly designing time, for his employment was after all as designer and not as dogsbody. Certainly if the client agrees to split the contract, design fees must be adjusted. Certainly split contracts, if there is time to control them properly, can work a perfection that may not other- wise happen. (In an ordinary straight contract where the contractor has sub-contracted, an error in that sub-contract may not reveal itself until site assembly when it cannot be removed and the designer must ad-hoc his design all round it. In a perfect split-contract job which the designer alone controls, there is the chance of spotting error at its inception and stopping any faulty delivery to site – though the blame is the designer's alone if he doesn't.)

Many companies have developed a compact, resonant company image which echoes through every piece of paper they put out. The resonance may run to a colour-scheme for the company itself, or perhaps to the association of colours with ranges of company product. It will almost certainly run to typefaces. It may even run counter to something you have been told at the initial briefing meeting.

In a case like this, where the compact image exists, it must have been mentioned at that meeting – by designer if not by client. The logic one looks for is that an exhibition stand, however much of a "special event" it may be, is nonetheless part of the client's practice. The stand should surely do in three dimensions what is more often done in two.

But there are other, more tentative motions clients will often make when this issue arises; and sometimes not so tentative either. "We don't want you running round to the advertising agency", you may be told: "Anything you want, you get in touch with us." The reasons for this are sometimes glaringly obvious – as that last year the advertising agency itself designed the stand and it "didn't work". This is quite likely. Used to working in two dimensions, addicted to "copy", anxious to get the image across in a world where exhibition designers often ignore it, the agency had gone beyond its competence and made a published book of the stand.

That the company believes in a corporate image is palpably clear from its printwork, and the same agency is known to be producing that printwork, almost certainly developing it further at this very moment. There is a contradiction here. The client has forbidden liaison between the designer and the agency. Yet at some other level the same client still retains that agency. Again the designer needs to develop his "sense of client", of who is saying what and for what precise reasons. He may very well be advised to go backstairs and meet the agency whatever has been forbidden him.

On the other hand, the reasons for shying away from an existing image, or failing to put one together, can be so blazingly stupid that one wonders how on earth the company failed to burn itself down long since. Inevitably, in studying the company's product, its exhibits, the designer meets sales-people; equally, in search of copy-lines, he meets copywriters from the advertising department; and very often indeed the two departments will be at a niggling sort of frontier war. Sales are going down, or not climbing enough, and he will be told that this is the fault of advertising; or the copy-writers will tell him that they are opening up new approaches which the salesmen will not change their habits to explore; and so on. This is murder for the independent freelance, who can be caught like a refugee between the two. Both sides will claim him of course. All he can do is dodge for cover under some other aspect of his brief, get back to the drawingboard and enter this problem of how much he can, or should, be continuing or helping to create a company image in the list of all the other problems now acting upon his design.

Valid reasons indeed exist for being "quite different". Quite apart from the traditional sense of celebration already noted, the client (and, for that matter, his advertising agency, his sales and advertising departments) may well be in search of a new public and a new market about which he knows little more than that being "the same" isn't finding it. Or the whole question of the rightness or wrongness of the existing image may be in debate, and an exhibition designed by a total outsider be a heavensent opportunity to alter the terms of argument.

Where no clarity of image exists the designer is of course freer, yet in the dark. Perhaps a factory process if not the product itself may start to spin a three-dimensional pattern into his thought. Or if that intractable domestic cube, which is sometimes refrigerator, sometimes boiler, sometimes TV set, sometimes washer, sometimes hi-fi unit, sometimes furniture, is customarily shown

'A process itself may start to spin a three-dimensional pattern into the designer's thought' (p. 63). The dog-eared rectangle forming all service cores to new dock installations (left) suggests a deep frame for pictures, exhibits and window-openings on the stand (above and over).

Designer: *Arthur Braven* for the Port of Liverpool

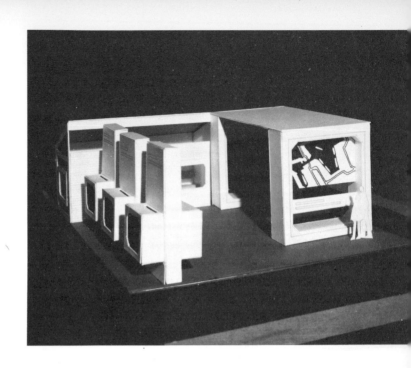

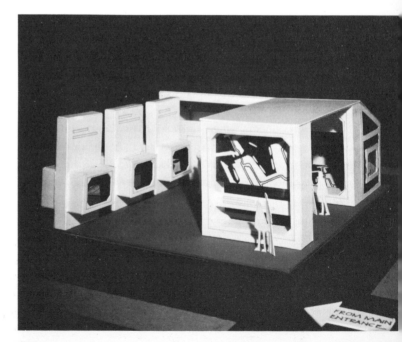

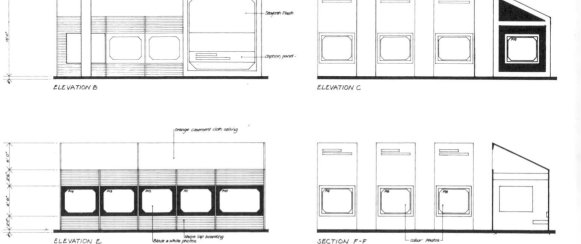

ELEVATION B

ELEVATION C

ELEVATION E

SECTION F-F

Left:
Without enclosing the stand completely, three flank "pillar" units effectively mask any possibility of neighbouring design confusing the image here – a fact easily demonstrated by turning the model, but not demonstrable by visual. (Chapter 13).

Above:
Part of a sheet of section details showing the service-core image shown on the previous page continued through the stand. Note also the economy of legend and that it runs well clear of drawn lines.

at the likely floor-levels of home, then now that the brief is to be "different" it should perhaps be suspended from the roof or sunk in the floor. The answers will be as surprising (and desperate) as the designers. But the breaks with custom, the actual "differences" proposed, have to fit with company intention. The designer has to know the client.

In that designer's goldmine of a book, *Printed Ephemera* by John Lewis, the definition of ephemeral is essentially of printwork produced for an ephemeral use: a railway ticket, a tobacco-pack label, are used and thrown away. Yet in the final dictionary sense of "existing only for a day, or for a few days" the fact that Lewis's examples begin some several days ago, in 1480, denies the word. He actually found the things! The designs continue to project themselves. Only the exhibition design is wholly ephemeral.

The proper parallel is theatrical. The brief is the plot; the organiser the lessee; a 3″ platform the stage; there are scene-builders, lighting experts, possibly even some prompting; infinite rehearsal with cuts and changes of emphasis in course; a dress rehearsal the night before that can stretch far into the small hours; and the designer, like the producer, operates on the *mise-en-scène*, the exhibits called actors, and the text itself. The play, as always, is the thing; but we are in fortnightly "rep" or "summer stock". Last week's play is forgotten, the one a fortnight hence is already in rehearsal, this one and that one must go on, just as all those others came off. Such poetic exegesis must be forgiven, for it is this extreme evanescence of exhibition design – the record of which, like the theatre's, is only found in the flat two-dimensional "lie" of photography – that makes for its huge excitement. One may, indeed one must (as I am informed), take bold decisions in fortnightly "rep" about the delineation of character, and stick with them, which by longer rehearsal, greater permanence, one would shade at the edges or graduate more subtly. This is because the time is less – to script, to rehearse, to play. It is also because the job is materially different: the impact sandwiched.

Consider, then, the materials.

For a start, nothing need be made to last because, however solid, it won't. Suppose you wish to show exhibits at floor-level but wish also to isolate them from too much handling or marking by visitors or because a stand-back view favours them. A convention would be to "island" them in areas on which no-one could walk. These might be filled with pebbles (common), the packed uneven off-cut ends of 2″ × 1″ and 2″ × 2″ wood (cheap in theory, but what did the contractor charge to do the packing?), clear glass marbles over light (but I believe that most of the marbles were stolen on that occasion), cat's cradle stringing or wiring (but mightn't unwary feet get caught?), water (but the evaporation rate in exhibitions is high, and the cigarette-butt fall is great), upended ends of rolls of corrugated paper (if they could be fire-proof).

This is only to speak of what, in some other situation or under the duress of longer runs, would be impractical either by an accumulation of dirt to ruin appearance or by an inherent fragility. But an exhibition stand has barely time to get dirty, and can be fragile. Exhibitors' three dimensional structures are impermanent. They need quick and distinct effectiveness. This puts a premium on materials that are extraordinary by being new in themselves, and these are very rapidly drawn into exhibiting's stock-in-trade: materials such as block polystyrene, metal foils, flat-colour photo processing were common here far earlier than elsewhere. So it is that the designer's response to new materials is less important than his ingenuity in the use of both old and new. The new ones will be flung at him anyway, and even if he should miss the salesman's call or fail to see the possibility in a trade announcement, the next exhibition he visits will bring him up to date, and this material like every other will simply become another in stock. What matters is a perpetual inquisitiveness which is the other side of that penny, ingenuity. No-one can propose an alternative use for a material the nature of which he hasn't studied. It is this, probing into materials to discover what potentialities they have, not what they have hitherto been used

69

for, that makes for most of the excitements exhibitions reveal: the wooden off-cuts, the marbles and so on.

Almost certainly however the exhibition designer would be well-advised to build up a library, not so much of treatises on design as of catalogues and reference information. New materials, new systems, new fittings would obviously have their shelf in this; but it is the duller, old-hat stock that gives the most: a timber merchant's list, that does not limit itself to 2″ × 1″, 2″ × 2″, 3″ × 1″, 6″ × 1″ and the rest, or that great tome from a foundry, less for the posts and simple channels one may have to employ than for the wealth of extraordinary sections that themselves suggest new angles of wall departure, or the fantastic perforated sheets that might themselves make walls. One trembles to think of the amount of costly custom-making for which the individual designer has been responsible which has, by fractions of an inch only, departed from cut lengths of standards.

Whether the vision comes first and the way to embody it follows, or whether the possible embodiments propel the vision, I don't know and it does not matter. What does matter is that knowledge of materials should be to hand; that specifications on a design should be precise.

Enormous importance attaches to how the design is first present-
ed to the client. An early form of presentation may be determined
by the client demanding a rough block-plan allocating space as
between office, display, stores and chief exhibits, or whatever are
to be the main components of his stand; and it is no bad rule to
supply such a block-plan anyway, whether demanded or not. In
total truth and in terms of design, it cannot mean much: domi-
nant elements that do not descend to ground-level or even head-
height will not show, but the "lie" is worth it. Signals like "drinks
cupboard", "main display wall", "storage", "platform display"
will be read and can at least be counted against the list of what
the client asked you to do; and it is a sort of insurance policy – as
much as to say "I am proceeding on these lines and, unless
stopped, will continue to do so." Essentially, however, the
problem is not one of blocking out against a brief but of how to
make real the designer's total treatment.

General current practice is to do this by visual: a fairly impos-
ing, sophisticated and fully-coloured two-dimensional picture,
sometimes accompanied by the sort of block-plan already suggested, sometimes by sketch elevations (especially for larger
projects) of other sides than that selected for full colour. The
trouble with this is that, as implied, it is all "lies" too.

Which face is in fact to be chosen for the full treatment? The
question answers itself for a gangway stand in a row presenting
only one face, and partly answers itself for a corner site where
both faces can get a look-in; but the answers aren't equally easy
for an island site, or for one that is very deep in which the inside
elevations looking outwards are likely to be at least as important
as the outside faces looking in, or for one where the brief has required that a large proportion of the space be enclosed – the
upper deck of a double-decker for instance – and where what
goes on inside the enclosure may be the most important thing the
designer has to cope with.

Moreover no exhibition stand face ever looks as it does in visual. If it is 9′ high to the top of the facia, then at the standback view implied by visuals the bottom 6′ are going to be obscured by people anyway; and you cannot stand that far back in any case except by standing on the back (or beyond) of the opposite exhibitor's stand and removing anything he may have built in the way. So what eye-view are you going to use – worm's? bird's? The answer is almost certainly going to be decided by nothing to do with the relative honesty or dishonesty of eye-heights. Suppose you wish to emphasise the relationship between some rear wall display and frontal fascia and other features. To do this your visual's slant is going to be the angle at which perspective frees that rear wall feature from the fascia line. It is no part of your design that visitors must either lie on the floor or stand on stilts to appreciate the stand, yet this is what is often enough – and for possibly very good reasons – implied. The huge "lie" incorporating such lesser "lies" is precisely that no exhibition stand is ever seen in situ in the total, isolated manner visuals suggest; and the virtuous design is not in fact the one that makes an elegant two-dimensional painting but the one which attracts the visitor – possibly from a distance – and then continues to hold his attention as he passes through a constantly changing series of relations of plane to plane, distance to proximity, and frequently interrupted spatial movement.

There are two enormous advantages of visualisation over every other form of presentation: because most designers use them they are expected by clients, and they are portable. And of course the portability matters. The visual can be posted from town to town and carted from office to Boardroom, from sales to advertising and back to sales, where it can and does sit on a filing cabinet and help the build-up towards the event. The client's roadmen will call in and see it, and the client's clients. It tells them practically nothing about the stand except that it will exist; but that, from the client's point of view, may well be more than nothing.

Nonetheless, presentation by scale-model is infinitely to be preferred to any coloured sketch. Certainly a model "lies" as a visual "lies", but not by one huge "lie" enclosing a lot of lesser ones. The scale – which for most stands can hardly be larger than $^1/_4''$ or $^1/_2''$ – falsifies the event, but within that scale everything is equally falsified. The relationship of fascia to rear wall (to pick on the same issue) is precisely as the model is tilted to show; the movements in spatial relations are true as one turns the thing; there are no suppositional walls, only the ones that are there.

Scale models have their disadvantages, it is true. The degree of detail to be shown is crucial – but then it is for visuals also – for too many tiny lines to indicate captions can muddle a presentation, the aim of which is clarity. In the same way, tiny patterns to indicate bold wallpapers had better be flat colour. And there is always that inability of most businessmen – however competent as map-reading motorists they may be – to think down-scale. ("I think", a Sales Director once said to me, putting his finger upon some modelled curtains, carefully simulated by wetting tissue-paper, "I think I would rather have curtains here than a paper effect.") Moreover models tend to break in transit from point to point, even if they are transportable without an attendant person. But their one supreme advantage is their relative truthfulness. A visual is likely to have put at centre (and quite sensibly) what the client has stated as being his most important exhibit, and so fix it centrally in the client's mind. A model, which will have done the same, will nonetheless have added the truth that from certain angles this central exhibit must be partially or totally obscured. The most constant complaint one hears from clients on site is "I thought this feature was to be equally prominent from all angles." In my experience one never hears it if presentation has been by model.

Essentially exhibitions are made in a rush. Everyone is always determined that this shall not be so next time, but it always is. The client may make his booking a year or more beforehand, and possibly brief his designer as much as six months ahead; but his product is going to change in such a length of time as half a year, or at least the angles by which it is to be sold are going to change. Design six months ahead of the event is going to be subject to heavy emendations. Suppose, as is more likely, that the brief is three months ahead, and the contract placed perhaps a month later. Since the range, intention and scope of stands vary so much, these kinds of general statement are dangerous to make; but in the same sweeping way there is a sort of nub-truth in saying that a stand's general structure – except of the most prestigious kind – is probably made over perhaps two weeks, its displays and furnishings over a longer period, and particular detailed features over a month or more.

Any one tradesman at work on one stand will almost certainly be at work on others – perhaps three or more – at the same time. A lot of his work will be by reflex. Flooring, ceiling, or simple runs of smooth-faced wall to receive display, will be made the way they are always made in his particular firm; and it doesn't really matter what detailed thought the designer may have given, or shown on his drawings, for such elements. A good exhibition drawing, in fine, is not the one containing every conceivable detail at equal weights of line and lettering, but the one locating the exceptional detail precisely – isolating it separately into a magnified detail if necessary. The exhibition draughtsman is not an architectural draughtsman. His craft lies not in seeing that everything is in but in deciding what can with safety be left out. Clarity on the workbench, for the painter, in the spray-shop, is what he is after.

Every plan the designer produces will of course contain its legend as well as its lines; but in the legend too this craft of omission matters. Both painter and carpenter – and indeed other

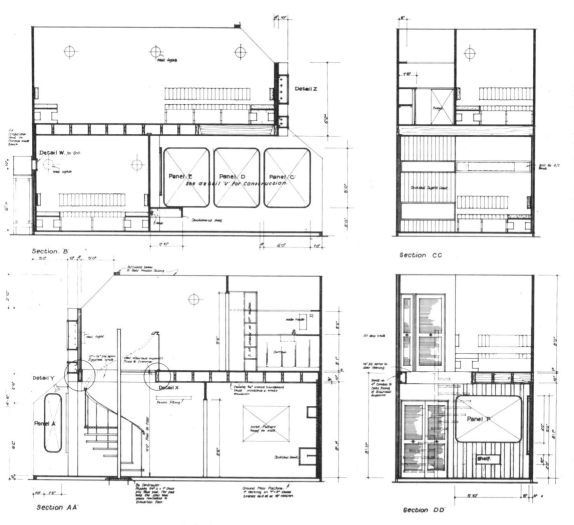

A single detail sheet containing all the elevations necessary for a small double-decker stand. Note the brevity and careful separation of legend from drawings throughout.

Designer: *Geoff Butcher*

craftsmen – will constantly refer to the same master drawing, so that any wording needs to be sufficiently isolated and specific for any craftsman to pick at once on the relevant instruction.

By simplification drawings tend to code themselves: open parallels tend to be walls: filled-in parallels, metalwork; speckling, carpets; rectangles crossed diagonally, applied display; close parallel lines, captions; and so on. But the corollary to this kind of symbolism is that the receiving contractor knows the designer's symbols. When he knows them – they are in fact pretty general, though not unfortunately universal – he will recognise what I have called the designer's "shorthand" and read and cost the drawings quickly. But it is of course unlikely that any four contractors in a competition will know each "shorthand" equally. Ideally there is no substitute for "talking" each contractor through the drawings, precisely to familiarise them with the drawing style, and one by one, since they will not always ask questions that might seem foolish before their competitors. And everything, however much you might expect it to be assumed, must be in the accompanying Specifications.

The designer's critical advantage in keeping the drawings skeletal, but the specifications full, is that his emphases are right and properly useful. It was on the carpenter's bench that a run of timber, which it was essential to the design should be unbroken, was in fact broken. Was the word "unbroken" clear and isolated enough? The designer's means is a simplicity of drawing, and a limitation of wording, so that the few words used have extra force.

The contract is placed. The job is in the works. But the whole job? Never, or practically never. Even for details bedded deep in the actual structural work, both designer and contractor may now be awaiting the client's pleasure. More likely there will be superficial display details to be fixed to a structural face. Almost certainly, the precise captioning will not have been fixed until the job is well in hand at works.

Common caution suggests therefore that the designer keeps an open mind as long as possible about the lettering size (though not the style) of captions, or the actual pattern by which doubtful quantities of his client's exhibits shall be fixed (though not the method of fixing). At the costing stage the matter will have been partly covered by Specifications, partly by a not very eloquent Display Sheet, giving the areas to be involved and such rough indications as "photo over-all", "photo and photoset caption", "client's exhibits fixed by client", "client's exhibits fixed by contractor by wiring", "not more than 50 colour pieces, each 6″ square, impact adhesive fix, with 4-figure applied letters as captions to each". What is most ill-advised is to draw at an early stage what you think will happen in any area of considerable doubt, for it almost certainly won't. What a contractor prices for and the designer then changes is likely to figure as extra work, whether the hours and materials involved seem to make it properly so or not. The designer has been as specific as possible, and provided he knows what the contractor's estimate has taken for, he can subsequently warn the client as to whether or not he is going over the top of it.

Essentially of course, from the designer's point of view, this sort of extrapolation of display from structure is a *bêtise*. The design is an entity incorporating captions, pictures, exhibits within its three dimensions. Nonetheless the extrapolation occurs: the client wants to change the words, the manufacturer changes the model shown to one of another shape; and though once more it is outside the function of this book, here is a factor constantly forcing upon the designer time and time again the big bold use of repeated shapes. If there are to be changes, let them be changes within shapes that are constant. If captions change by hundreds of words in length, then let at least the caption board not change – the 12″ circle, it may be – and let the style remain white out of black or whatever it was the original conception dictated; and, finally, let that style be one that can be easily repeated in haste. Nothing of course is very well proofed against such a disaster as a sudden multiplication in the number, for instance, of leaflets to be shown, which can splutter all over an otherwise impeccable job like blots on paper. The designer can only have tried to allocate and limit specific areas within the design in which the chaos happens. If he is witty, if he has guessed his client's quirks correctly, he has so disposed things that the design can contain even that rash of literature. If he is lucky, such dispositions are largely out of sight. Only if he is blessed will his client be the one – and not one of the other ninety-nine – whose company will not change its mind.

PART FOUR   THE CLIENT'S OBJECT

16   ON SITE

The designer's role on site is hard to script, but it must include some general moves. He will keep the client, who has fathered the thing and might by now be thoroughly neurotic, away from site. Indeed if things are working well this may become virtually his sole occupation. The more experienced client, before an exhibition that has a six or seven day period for set-up, will probably not turn up until the last two days in any case; but the inexperienced will haunt the place and fuss both themselves and others. Even the experienced, when they do turn up, suffer from fits of over-optimism and start marching up and down the gangway, head down, scowl up, long before any possibility of completion. There may, after all, be plenty to disturb the inexperienced simply in the chaos of any exhibition in process of erection. Anything the designer can do to put his mind at rest is well worthwhile: there may be real anxieties ahead, and no sense at all in setting them afloat on a quite unnecessary previous irritation.

The designer will also not himself march up and down like a desperately expectant father, suggesting nothing so much to the craftsmen before him as the expectation of disaster. Instead he can double-check whatever arrangements he has made – that those late captions will be here at noon tomorrow, or that the suspension wires for the roof will be slung and ready for his own contractor by first thing in the morning. Or he will take the contractor aside from the stand for a moment to double-check that a schedule agreed between them is running smoothly – for if it isn't, better by far the designer should know of this than have it sprung on him by a client nosy enough to have discovered it first. He will watch for his own particular worries of course: that power-feed under the floor, for instance, especially if his drawings were in the end over-loaded with other instructions. Once the floor is down, such a feed will have to come down from the roof and be unsightly, or over the floor like an obstacle race.

He will go away as much as possible, but he will leave a note

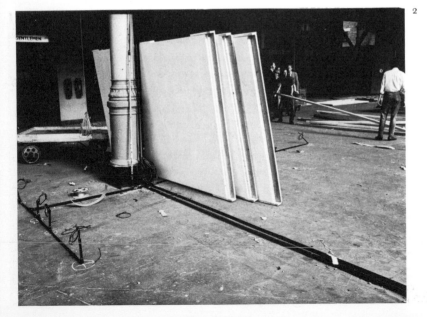

This sequence of pictures illustrates the erection on site of a small stand and indicates the kinds of problem designers may meet.

1 The original sketch model. The site is poor, one short side only being on a main gangway, and containing a building pillar. The rear wall, clear of roofs, can "signal" to a wide range of gallery angles. Late amendments will include extra supports to the 'flying' roofs in the interests of economy, and revised display to the "tower" which is the stand's service and storage core as well as masking the pillar.

2 Once flooring is laid over it the electricity supply cannot be shifted.

3 The designer has arranged for the neighbouring stand's contractor to build the party wall of stock-panels – an economy to both clients. This is quickly up, but not yet stable. Since the front of the stand is fixed by the building pillar, an error in chalk-out has introduced a ditch at the back to be filled and carpeted – an "extra" economies can pay for.

3

against emergency of where he is. He will take the client away, perhaps on a tour of the show in the process of set-up, mindful that there is nothing so cheering to clients as signs of despair on rival stands – unless it be the fortification of food and drink. Neither he nor client is the kind of craftsman on whom the care of this precious object now depends, and both of them are best a long way off, and even sedated, except at certain key moments. Certainly he should ask the contractor if his presence is wanted, and accept the contractor's answer within reason. There will be cases, especially when revisions have been late, when things might be expected to go wrong because underinformation will be rife. There may not, for instance, be an organiser's rubber-stamp approval on some particular polystyrene job for there might have been too little time to submit for approval. Even then, instead of lurking, the designer who knows what he is about would be better employed in seeking out the organiser, his consulting engineer, the fire prevention officer or anyone else who might conceivably become involved and getting, man to man, a clearance before some mischance has got someone's hackles up and his matchbox out – for even fireproof polystyrene doesn't like a flame – and a great deal of soothing propitiation and even repair-work has become necessary.

If the drawings were right, if the specifications were right, if the proper approvals have been sought and found, if the contractors have a schedule for delivery on site and there's no reason to suppose they cannot keep it, if the client's exhibits are arriving at such-and-such a time and the client shortly afterwards, if all the constituent parts feel right, a visit to site should be little more than a courtesy except where someone calls for it. But if those earlier ifs have not been fixed, if progress at works has not looked consequential, if the contractor has seemed too easily and too often to say "yes yes" at every point at which you might have expected to hear some doubt, or if you are uncertain about the clarity in drawing or specification, then indeed there is plenty to worry about, and you will lurk. For what else is there now for you to do save be on hand – however bad this is for everyone else's morale, however much advice you receive to the contrary, however much you, rather than your client, are worrying now? But if on hand, it is to be usefully so. What in these cases will be at fault may not, it is true, be your design – though it may be a fault in your progress of your design – so much as a failure by the contractor or a client's impossibly late demand; but snags that arise in your presence are yours as designer to solve. If you have not that very special knack of inventive emergency wit, then stay away and pray the contractor has.

4 Structures on the neighbouring stand are now fixed, and stabilise, the rear wall on which work can begin at once.

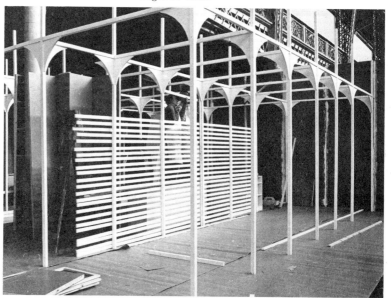

5

6

7

5, 6 & 7 The rear wall is now painted and units delivered from works. Prefabricated sections can now be assembled quickly and painted, and prefabricated displays fixed to them.

8 The revised "tower" display involves using client's existing lightboxes. Because of the building pillar these cannot be recessed, and must therefore stand proud of the building line. A last-minute permission is required to permit this.

9 The fixing of client's own exhibits complete the stand, the ultimate justification for which (over) must be whether its abrupt variations in ceiling height and colour draw the eye across and through other stands and encourage visitors in along the rear wall displays.

Contractor, Trident Displays Ltd; Photos, Lance Browne.

Before entering this eleventh hour of possible confusion, one must at once admit that the exhibitor with desperate last-minute requests does not stand in for every industrial exhibitor the world over; but he will do for a great many of them. Nor is this to be merely captious.

While the designer has been racing against the clock to make sure that tomorrow morning his part of the brief, his vision by picture or model and working drawings, shall be realised, the client too has been involved in a race against time that has almost certainly been infinitely more complex to run, and not with individuals as in the designer's case, but with factories and capital investment and such related details as print programmes of promotional material. The chances of his having missed the boat, depending upon whether his company is great or small and commands vast or pathetic resources, are thus decisively higher. Particularly, problems rooted in the close relationship, in many fields of industrial exhibiting, to product launching are endemic to exhibitions. Important exhibits simply don't turn up, or turn up quite different in height, bulk, weight and colour to anything for which anyone has been prepared.

To some extent one might have recognised a warning signal early on – some phrase at a briefing meeting, such as "We shall be exhibiting something still in prototype only" – and having recognised it, design to meet this contingency in the sense of providing an open space with brilliant general lighting rather than a spotlit plinth, which may in the event prove too small, too weak, and with wrongly directed light. One can also pass the danger signals on. The contractor ought to be warned, for example, that in some particular area, signwriter, painter and electrician might be wanted for possible emergency; and the organiser (and possibly the Unions too) that late-night working might be inevitable if they will please permit it. Typeset and photo-time might be booked as well against a rush of after-opening captions.

Somewhere in every exhibition hall towards the end of set-up flurries of panic show. Because a take-over bid has been clinched on the market, people whom the designer has never met, may suddenly descend on his stand with enormous unmatching banners announcing "Now a Member of the . . . Group". A vast exhibit, extra to any ever listed, has suddenly turned up. The client sent the contractor the 1970 pattern-book in error, and all 12′ of that wall of colour patches must now be stripped bare to receive the 1971 range which has just arrived. The working model with the power-feed is not exhibit G but exhibit H, where there is no power; but you cannot switch them round for the captions are backlit and wired and already built into the walls. They've decided to show that new feed, not as cake for pigs, but pellets for geese and want a new caption reading "Christmas is coming and the . . ." in red and green, with holly round it. The company logo has been changed, so stick this over that wherever it occurs, and if that is bigger then paint it out.

This is an interesting moment. The thing looks good, or not. You have sensed – what is not easy for men with other trades and preoccupations to communicate – what the three-dimensional image proper to them should be; and here is what you have provided. The thing looks good, or not – but to others rather than to yourself.

The obvious precautions have been taken earlier in the morning, or with luck, which you need as well as good management, the night before. Emergency work outside the contract as placed has been itemised, signed for as "extras", and done or will be done at times you can assert. The stand has been swept and cleaned of its inevitable thumbprints. In your wisdom, or in the contractor's wisdom, despite the public address announcement "All contractors out of the building now" as much as an hour ago, you have perhaps kept a man with hammer and nails handy for minor additions, and perhaps another with a sheet of the nearest matching Letraset and a touch-up brush.

The fact is that members of the client's company will often arrive even as late as this with items to fix, of which you have never heard: sales charts, proofs of a particularly encouraging company report, the "odd bottle" and glasses though these were long ago ruled out, samples of something "in the pipeline" they cannot yet publicly advertise (though they might have done to you) but wish to show discreetly. These are usually, and blessedly, for that enclosed or office area which clients often in these ways manage to turn into what seems a kind of mess in which they feel at home. And there is from time to time that catastrophic type of client who does not like the object you have provided him, exactly matched as it may be to visual, model, working drawings, who asks for additions now, and persists in phoning your studio almost daily hereafter for more additions or alterations right up to the end of the exhibition, and whose efforts increasingly spoil and muddle and diffuse the intended impact. With such a one you can only insist that all these bits and bobs of captions, flower-bowls, colouring, arrows – he has a passion for arrows – are each one an "extra" and allow them only against his signature. He is inevitably, so it happens, the one who will query the eventual billing where the bits and bobs will figure as bobs and quids. But the plain fact is that he does not understand the nature of exhibitions. Here is the object of a lengthy exercise by himself, the contractor and yourself and this is now what he has to use. Additions will not help him.

The major catastrophe is not this kind of unseasoned nuisance but the veteran's disfavour. By and large my experience is that clients accept on the day what is after all in large part the creation of their own company. There may have been from the beginning, perhaps the result of asking for "something different", the danger that once the object was handed to them they would feel uneasy with it. They might always hitherto have had a totally enclosed and private office area, for instance, but have asked for this to be opened up in some way so that the visitor could see, but not interfere with, the company at work. You may therefore have made their office merely an open space at a higher or lower level, since there is nothing like three steps up or down to inhibit the casual visitor; or you may have provided "walls" of slatted display between each slat of which they can be seen at work beyond. Only now is it apparent to them that they cannot here create a sort of cosy mess without grave injury to the intended impact of the over-all design. An initial unease of this sort can become fixed, can be appreciative but suggest some changes for the next time round, can even transform itself into a conscious delight once the new "feel" of the thing becomes established. Only the very veteran and major exhibitors brief their stand-staff, possibly calling the designer in to help, about why the design is the way it is and how it is intended it should work; and it is therefore no waste of the designer's time to make the moment of handover a fairly detailed tour of his own intentions, a kind of briefing to salesmen which probably hasn't been given and which there is no-one else so well-informed to give.

This is the last conceivable figure in the designer's exercise; and it is important in another way. With all the talk he has heard from the start about the company's operation, the intention behind the stand, the peculiar difficulties inherent in presenting this particular product, this is possibly his only chance of an appreciation in active, human terms. Here are the men and women who actually have to sell the goods and talk the message across. It is no bad thing, in terms of future thinking about design for them, to stay and listen and hear them at it, and no bad thing to get to know them either – for it is a consummation most devoutly to be wished that there will be future design, and for these people precisely. The object is no longer the designer's in any very real sense, but theirs to be happy with or hate.

There has seemed to me no other way to write this book than to pick on typical influences upon the designer in the sort of sequence in which experience suggests they might arise: a dangerous course, containing at least as many "lies" as an exhibition visual. One can with truth no more extract one exhibition's course from the designer's life than a battle from a war. The falsities come everywhere. It may even be that some designer somewhere has never had an awkward client. Most have had many.

But the major untruth in this kind of isolation of any one job is that even in such swingeing terms as I have used, the designer's situation is never that of a job at a time.

Two dozen small to medium sized stands in a year is a total below which the freelance can hardly afford to fall. But are these one or two a month briefed, or visualised, or work-drawn, or completed, or started at works? One stand may be finished, but what of the other one back on the drawing board? Or the one which goes on site next week? Or that heap of drawings back from costings and now demanding economies in structure? What about that waiver from the organisers for Client X? That special fixing detail for Contractor Y? The designer cannot, in fact, dictate his flow of work.

The joy of exhibition work – one comes back again and again to the same few images – is its theatricality: the speed with which things happen, particularly the speed that means they have got to happen now, that this emergency contrivance has got to be it because curtain goes up in an hour, and the inspired accidents that are bred of such immediate pressures. The designer has to like all that, or bust. He has also to like the immediacy of work in another sense: the directness of going over the drawing with precisely the man who will make from it, the possibility that some new and extraordinary effect will develop there and then as he does so. And that in turn – though some superb designers look as austere and toplofty as some theatrical stars – means a certain gregarious pleasure in the company, at the making end, of the skilled and even the cack-handed who will make or mar his work. And even that, chase it back to its beginnings, means a certain inquisitiveness, nosiness, suspiciousness about the weird back passages and inner-company as well as inter-company warfares, and the other vagaries between factory and fairground that call themselves Industry.

The business is exciting: full of loud-mouth, disaster, rescue, success unbelievable, showiness, full of effects and extraordinary people. And then the show comes off, is largely forgotten in the whole furore of getting another one going somewhere else. It is full of eleventh hours, last minutes, whopping generalisations, exquisite detail. But mostly it is a permanent one o'clock in the morning, full of the witching hours which are just behind you. You love the whole unmappable jungle. And just occasionally, as I have been informed – indeed as I dimly remember – you toy with the idea of a return to civilisation, and you reject it.